Grace Ellery Channing

Sea Drift

Poems

Grace Ellery Channing

Sea Drift
Poems

ISBN/EAN: 9783744704403

Printed in Europe, USA, Canada, Australia, Japan

Cover: Foto ©Thomas Meinert / pixelio.de

More available books at **www.hansebooks.com**

SEA DRIFT

POEMS BY
GRACE ELLERY CHANNING

SCIRE·QVOD
SCIENDVM

Boston
Small, Maynard & Company
1899

PRESS OF
Rockwell and Churchill
BOSTON, U.S.A.

TO MY FATHER

CONTENTS

I

II

III

"WHO GO DOWN TO THE SEA IN SHIPS."

The written thought, the printed word,
  Are ships that sail the sea;
And Time, the ocean, gives account
  Of many an argosy.

Some safe with merchandise make port
  That lowly ventured thence,
Nor ever steered them by a thought
  Beyond mere opulence.

And some, the stateliest embassies
  That ever filled the eye,
With song and band that left the land,
Veiled ones, who watch and understand,
  Tell where their fragments lie.

Some are the mighty liners;
  Where the long sea-surge rolls,
Through storm and night, through sun and light,
They carry safe in all despite
  Their cabin-lists of souls.

And some wherever keel may grate
  Or prow may cut the foam
Are pilots of the treacherous waves,

Through piled-up years, through years of graves,
 Bringing the millions home.

Some are fair pleasure craft that bore
 White sails into the sun,
Catching the momentary light, —
A day's gay dance, then the long night
 When the gay dance is done.

And some on deeds of mercy fare
 And some on deeds of war; ·
With grim, great cannon set to kill,
Or kind gold grain to feed and fill
 Life that was Death's before.

But most — (Make light thy breath to these,
 O winds of Destiny!) —
Are fisher boats that plough the seas
Oh, not for happy Isles of ease,
Nor gold fruit of Hesperides,
But bread, bread from the hungry seas,
For children at their mothers' knees
 And mothers yet to be!

Loud laughs that sea with tempest;
 Boats are its boisterous sport;
Ten million have set boldly forth
 And ten are come to port.

Oh, well the mariner may stand
For a bold course and true;
A ship well manned, a voyage well planned,
If he will sail it through!

And happy is that mariner
And voyage, whate'er its start,
When the long *molo* is well past
Who finds the anchor holding fast,
The light shine in the dark at last,
And harbour in some heart!

Yet, for the voyage is glorious,
The great sea wide and free,
Up, coward anchor! — Set the sail! —
Steer for the open! — Should Time fail,
Remains Eternity!

WAR

The great Republic goes to war,
But Spring still comes as Spring has done,
And all the Summer months will run
Their summer sequence as before;
And every bird will build its nest,
The sun sink daily in the west,
And rising eastward bring new day
In the old way.

But ah, those dawns will have a light,
Those western skies burn golden bright,
  With what a note the birds will sing,
  And Winter's self be turned to Spring
    Than any Springtime sweeter far,
    When once again, calm entering,
      The great Republic comes from war!

PITY, O GOD

Pity thy deaf, O God! — thy helpless deaf,
Only whose ears perceive the music's birth;
The fair, glad, mirthful melodies of earth
Or sea, or wind-kissed trees in forest dim;
Life's morning anthem, Nature's vesper hymn;
The hum of bees about a bursting flower,
The blithe down-patter of a summer shower,
The lull of water and the lisp of wave,
Or rush of sea-foam from some sea-bound cave;
The wafted breeze, whose airs æolian
Murmurously rise and murmurous die again;
The tender cry of bird that shuns the light
      For joy, not dole;
Or the Belovèd's voice on moonlit night,
      Whereat dead hearts rise whole;
Who hear these sounds, but only with the ear, —
Whose souls are deaf, — make them, O God, to
      hear!

Pity thy blind, O God! — thy sightless ones,
Unseeing, whose purblind eyes alone left free
Behold the limitless and changing sea,
The heaven of stars, the power in beauty furled,
The sun-illumined and cloud-shadowed world,
The day adorned and night magnificent;
The meadows with a million flowers besprent;
The fields all warmed, caressed, and played upon
By the great, glowing, lavish lover, Sun,
Bathed in drenched clouds, swept by the airs of
    heaven,
Evening to morn, and morning until even;
The dim, sweet gardens where the langourous
    roses
    To swoon begin;
Or the Belovèd's face, when twilight closes
    And shuts sweet Love within;
Who sees these only with the eyes' dull light, —
Whose souls are blind, — O God, give them
    their sight!

Pity thy dumb ones, God! — thy speechless ones,
Only whose tongues free and unfettered are;
Whose lips the secret of the morning star
Hath ne'er unlocked; — no wingèd word of fire,
No fancy and no freedom, no desire
Thrilled from the throat in song, — stolen from
    the fingers

In subtler speech which burns and glows and
     lingers
Through thousand forms wherein divinely
     wrought
Into divinest life divinest thought
Stands fashioned; whom the Pentecostal flame
Hath never touched; in whom nor joy nor shame
Nor liberty, nor truth's self clearest shown
     Hath utterance stirred;
Nor the Belovèd's heart upon their own
     Wooed forth one whispered word;
Speechless, whose tongues speak only, — make
     them whole,
O God, unseal the dumb lips of their soul!

Pity thy poor, O God! — thine outcast ones,
Thy poor, who only are not poor of gold;
Who have no part in all the stores untold,
The largesse that a liberal Past hath lent;
No wealth of power, no riches of content,
No jewelled thoughts riven from the rarest
     mine;
No pleasure-palaces of fancy fine;
No gardens fair where sweet caprice may wander;
No lavish hoard of happiness to squander;
No halls of hope; no peaceful green domains;
No brooks of joy nor golden-memoried plains;

No holy temple guarding its white portal
   For one Belovèd Guest;
No consecrated feast whose cup immortal
   Love's lip hath prest;
Who have but gold, — dear God, how poor they
   be;
The beggared souls; succour their poverty!

AWARDS

A hero's crown for that man of men
   Whose right arm shall prevail!
But what befits their prowess then,
What laurels shall their brow attain,
What guerdon to their lot remain,
   And what hosannas hail,
Who fail and fail and fail again,
   And rise again — to fail?

A SONG OF THE SINGER

Like a sweet bird, as swift and soft of wing;
   Like a still cloud an unseen wind doth move
   Like a remembered twilight dream; like Love
When first Love stirs and hidden heart-strings
     sing;
   The violet-lidded Spring
Hath stolen in unseen 'twixt night and day;

There hath not been a change in anything ;
Only the lucent amber of the air,
Only an amaranth the mountains wear,
  Only a something that no man can say,
      Doth silently declare
The unchanged earth is changed and grown
          more fair ;
      And perfumes witnessing
The passing of the purple-stolèd Spring
      Do fragrantly convey
That Spring, sweet-lidded Spring, hath passed
      this way.

And I, who am come back with her as one
Strayed out of Greece, when white-armed Greece
          was young
  (Strayed out of Greece by way of Galilee),
Lute in my hand as when the whole world sung,
And wandered all the centuries adown,
      — Still with the olive crown, —
Stand sudden dazed and dumb, strayed in
          among
A frantic crowd in a disordered scene,
Warring with giant woes and wants obscene.
What do I here, out of my forests green,
      A singer among men,
With naught to do but sing old songs again ;

A ghost unlaid,
Who has outstayed Time's dawn, outstripped
Time's shade;
Astray in a strange land,
Songs on my lips and lute within my hand?

Yea, what do I, astray out of the years,
Who have outlingered Greece and Palestine,
And in the world have nothing that is mine
Save a heart heavy with its unshed tears
And lute that no man hears?
The heart all human and the lute divine;
The heart from Palestine, the lute from Greece;
The lute that cannot give the full heart ease;
The heart that to the lute's sweet revelry
Pours out its tears for wine.
I caught the lute up when his hand let fall, —
The last, least Grecian singer of them all, —
Though small, 'twas large enough for me;
I twined it round with deathless eglantine;
But the heart on a hill in Palestine
Some one had dropped — I found it, made it
mine;
How heavy hearts can be,
I could not know, but ever since I wear it
achingly.
O misplaced heart,

That in the lute song taketh no glad part!
    O lute mistuned,
That sounding joy and bliss doth only wound!
    O twain that be
Forever sounding, ever out of harmony!

And even so are we — the World and I;
    For who that lieth racked with mortal pains,
    Or hath the palsied Winter in his veins,
Will lift glad eyes to see the Spring go by?
    'Tis Winter if he die.
Or cares outside what living airs may bless;
If amaranth or dun the shadows lie;
    Or in what golden sunlight olives bow
    Their silver salutations down; nor how
Over grey walls the throbbing roses press
And gold-green lizards dance for happiness; —
    'Tis bitter foolishness!
As foolish I, finding no better part
Than crying " Joy! " to an unjoying heart;
Bearing old messages; to dying men
Singing old, empty, idle songs again
    That ease no pain: —
How I have wandered through
The earth, and birds sing as they used to do;
    Also how I have seen,
And in the forests still the trees are green;

O World, O Heart, O Fate,
Singer and song a thousand years too late!

ENGLAND

Who comes to England not to learn
    The love for her his fathers bore,
Breathing her air can still return
    No kindlier than he was before? —
In vain, for him, from shore to shore
Those fathers strewed an alien strand
    With the loved names that evermore
Are native to our ear and land.

Who sees the English elm trees fling
    Long shadows where his footsteps pass,
Or marks the crocuses that Spring
    Sets starlike in the English grass,
    And sees not, as within a glass,
New England's loved reflection rise,
    Mists darker and more dense, alas!
Than England's fogs are in his eyes?

And who can walk by English streams,
    Through sunny meadows gently led,
Nor feel, as one who lives in dreams,
    The wound with which his fathers bled —
    The homesick tears which must, unshed,

Have dimmed the brave, unfaltering eyes
    That saw New England's elms outspread
Green branches to her loftier skies?

How dear to exiled hearts the sound
    Of little brooks that run and sing!
How dear, in scanty garden ground,
    The crocus calling back the Spring
    To English hearts remembering!
How dear that aching memory
    Of cuckoo cry and lark's light wing!
And for their sake how dear to me!

Who owns not how, so often tried,
    The bond all trial hath withstood;
The leaping pulse, the racial pride
    In more than common brotherhood;
    Nor feels his kinship like a flood
Rise blotting every dissonant trace? —
    He is not of the ancient blood!
He is not of the Island race!

London, 1898.

HEAVEN OR HELL

O Soul, our day on earth is done,
We are failing with the fading sun;
To-morrow's, rising, shall behold
An empty tenement and cold,
Deserted, tenantless, and bare,
Which thou and Life so long did share,
And, Soul, we shall be wandering — where?
In what strange land, to what strange doom,
Awakes the Sleeper from the tomb?
  O Soul, consider well,
  Dost merit Heaven or Hell?

We've sinned, my Soul; in every way
Our wayward wills have gone astray;
No uncommitted fault, no thought
Of evil, but we two have wrought;
We've sinned, alas! — yet, Soul, be brave;
Disputeless claim to Heaven we have,
For it a heaven here we gave:
We loved, were loved; for fear of sin
We starved Love till he died within,
 We conquered mightily.
 Heaven the reward shall be.
  O Soul, — a sudden fear, —
  Go humbler here!

What if at last in some dread place
We see a judging Angel's face,
With fainting, trembling eyes, that seek
Our doom ere the divine lips speak?
And what if then, O Soul, we see
Adjudged by that august decree
Our sin, O Soul, our sin to be
Nor this, nor that; no one of all
The slips we counted each a fall;
But, sin all sins above,
The pride which murdered Love?
          Soul, dying eyes see well:
          Heaven, loveless, will be — Hell.

LUCIFER

"Let him that hath been wronged salute thee!"
George Sand.

I am the Angel of the fallen Star:
Men say I lost it from the angelic crown
That burned my guilty forehead when adown
From the infinite heights of Heaven I plunged
    afar
Into eternal Hell; — lo, on that star,
Once diademed, my regnant feet are set!
I did not lose, only I scorned to wear;
Another and more glorious past compare
Awaits me, but it has not risen yet.

No star shines bright enough to light my brows;
I have cast my crown from me — Love allows
No crown his consecrated brows above,
Save Love's own scarred insignia : *I am Love*,
And crownless greater than the crowned ones
are.

I am the patient Angel: — round me swing
A million worlds of souls ; incessant flights
Of lesser ministrants, to calmer heights
Pass by; — I see them pass; — each aspirant
wing
Upbearing a pale soul aspiring
With love-expectant eyes; — I bend my own.
Aeons like butterflies flit pass ; alone
Upon my star I hold my post and wait.
Like sombre shadows of some brooding fate,
From either mighty shoulder straight outspread
My ominous wings; — the living and the dead,
Born and unborn, who yet shall be and are,
I, Lucifer, lord of the fallen Star,
Wrap close beneath the darkness of my wing.

I am the infinite Angel. Who of all
The angelic host forsook high Heaven for hell ?
Man's angelhood who ever loved so well,
From angel state consentingly to fall ?

Not the joy-bringing angels — them ye call
Guardians; not dark Death with the dread pall;
Not he sublimely broken on the Cross
(The loving Angel!) who for Man would die.
These loved indeed, yet loved not these as I,
Who for Love's sake bear love's eternal loss.
Hell! blind one, Heaven's gate lies close within;
And for the sombre suffering men call sin,
Look up! — that far, faint, radiant gleam above
The forehead of the high, sad Angel, — Love,
Lucifer, — whom thou hatest most of all.

WHEN COMES THE SAD YEAR

When comes the sad year to its close
    And leaves fall fast about thee — think:
In other gardens summer glows,
    And others, thirsting, breathe and drink
The perfume of the rose;
Bethink thee, even in thy snows.

And when thy rose is blossoming — know,
    Though thine laugh in its leafy crown,
    In other gardens, stripped and brown,
    At other feet dead leaves fall down,
Dead roses lie beneath the snow;
Remember, when thine bud and blow.

WHY DOST THOU DOUBT

It is enough: thy sky's unclouded; there's a
　　boundless blue
　Above those hills; that breath of perfumed
　　air
Swept o'er thy flowers.　Shall it not be true
　That Thou art, O Thou ever loving Care
　　To whom my thirsting heart turns long-
　　ingly?

Deep silence: not one whispered sound to tell
　　me if I reach
　Truthward or no; the stillness gives no sign.
And yet — and yet, may not that stillness
　　teach
　How safely Earth rests in a calm divine?
　　Greatness alone so very still could be.

Horizonwards, with glorious banners, glows the
　　Sun-God, and drops.
　So day is dead: — O what if Heaven be far!
The dusk is purple on the mountain tops,
　And o'er them (O my heart!) the rising Star.
　It is enough — enough.

O PATIENT SUN

O patient Sun, which shinest daily down
  Such lives, such scenes, such levels of content,
And yet doth not disdain to shine, — shine on :
  And light a radiant world to high ascent!

Compassionate, send thy warm beams abroad,
  Kindle a generous fire in frost-chilled lands ;
Nourish the hungry nations ; give reward
  Of harvest to brown hands.

Lift up the drowsy lids of dreaming flowers ;
  Burn in the rainbow tints of darting wings ;
Smite the dull Earth with gladness ; gild grey
    hours,
  Till Winter's glow like Spring's.

Send thou a laughing sunbeam through wide
    space
  Past leering roofs, in alleys dank and cold,
To glad one little child, with glimmering grace
  To dance above the mould.

Then send thy great sweet Angel down, O
    Mother!
  Saying : " I poured my golden gifts for all ;
Shall man for man do less, brother for brother? "
  O patient Sun! — for still thy sunbeams fall.

TO A YOUNG METEOROLOGIST

ON HIS BIRTHDAY

Dear wanderer of the skies — to-day
I send a messenger thy way
  To track thee unawares ;
Adventurer of cloudy seas,
I send Love's self with wings, and these,
  My loving hopes and prayers :

The Fate that framed thy visions high,
And set thy glances in the sky,
  Be prophet of thy days ;
That through life's stress and storm and wrack
Men's eyes may mark thy starry track
  In wonder and in praise.

Thou who wouldst rule the upper ocean,
Give fetters to its giant motion,
  Compel its boundless course, —
Oh, be as boundless, thou ! Include
In thine own soul its every mood,
  Its passion and its force.

The eddying tides, the ebb and flow,
The heat and cold, the fire and snow,
  That in its bosom brood ;

The devastating surges ; — pen
Them all within thy spirit, then
    Be ruler of that flood !

Drawing the lightning from the skies,
Oh, be thyself unto men's eyes
    As lightning swift to dart,
And as the thunderbolt to smite,
Whenever clouds obscure the Right,—
    Strike through the Evil's heart !

And as the winds thou wouldst enchain,
Breathe through the world thyself again
    A purifying breath ;
A healing breeze, where Earth hath need,
Cyclonic, when she shall be freed
    From seeds of ill and death.

Be as the tempest terrible,
And as the storm-sky powerful,
    And as the lightning sure ;
But like that sky, the tempest done,
Pour forth thy love, as it the sun,
    As calm and high and pure.

So, passing as the meteor's flight
From unknown night to unknown night,
    Leave this undying fame :

" He bowed the heavens in his hand ;
Mightier, — he lifted up his Land
   Nearer to Heaven's frame."

JUDGMENT

A dead Soul lay in the light of day,
   Desperate, wan, it had passed ;
Oft foiled, it had toiled on its upward way
   Till it perished, spent, aghast,
After a thousand defeats the prey
   Of its conquering sin at last.

Said a stranger : — " Lo, how in shame and woe
   Is Satan's seal ever set ! "
Laughed a foe : — " Doth the carrion lie so low?
   Death and a coward well met."
Said a friend : — " His strength was great, I
     know,
   But his weakness was stronger yet."

Moaned his love unwed : — " Peace to the dead ;
   And as God shall forgive — let be ! "
But an Angel spread o'er the prostrate head
   His wings in humility ;
As he gazed : — " Be praised, Great God," he
     said,
   " For a glorious victory ! "

WINGS

A dream of wings,
A vision and a sound of flying things:
Sweet wings of song, fleet wings of hurrying
　　hours,
Joy-plumèd moments, glories, triumphs, powers,
　Golden and swift and sudden as day dying;
And heavy wings of sorrows, trailing low
Their sombre fringe; and blinding wings that go
Whirling some flashing joy; slow wings of pain
That languid beat the air and still remain
　Forever poised for flight, but never flying;
　　　Dwellers in dear green trees
　　　Are winged like these.

I dream of wings:
The restless stir, the feathered fluttering
Of hope, too feeble yet for wandering;
(Unsafest fledgling! tarry in the nest;
Leaving, thy plumes are arrows for some breast.)
The hovering, spread pinions opaline
Of an upbearing faith, steady, serene,
And jubilant and tireless and strong,
Whose song is flight, whose stalwart flight is
　　song,
From the first lifting, tiny, feathered curl
Of the nesting dreamer to the splendid furl

Of resting wings on wings, in gathering mood
For farther flight into infinitude;
Then how they leave, they lift, they rise, they
    bear —
Wings of the air, like these, — wings of the air,
Eagle and gull, — Oh, what a flight is there!

    I dream of wings:
Butterfly wings of fancies; gossamer,
Airier still, of subtle shapes that stir
And wake and breathe, one flickering hour to
    spread
Ephemeral gauzes forth, and then be dead, —
    Yet winged, still wingèd were in their brief
    staying;
And small, soft wings that dip and hush and
    hover,
    That bend and brood and cover
    Still smaller, softer, lowlier featherlings,
And breast to breast on the belovèd's laying,
    With crooning, warbling, singing,
That warmer, lighter, safer, closer press,
The nearer, dearer for the nakedness;
Warm wings of love, that fold and hold and bless
With feathered touches, feather-soft caress;
    Such high song, lowly winging,
      Such peace, such bliss, such rest,
      Have dwellers of the nest.

I dream of wings :
Weak wings and wistful, stormy wings and
      strong,
Plumes shod with music, feather-sandalled song,
Sweeping the air-ways of the sky along ;
Quick-throbbing, wide, vibrating, life-filled, free,
Messengers many as the winds that be,
The universe is but a nest for ye.
And dimly I discern within the weaving
Of wings with wings, the blue still intercleaving,
Wings and more wings ; — till folded calm
      without,
Beyond the darkness and beyond the doubt,
Past the believing and the unbelieving,
Warm, safe, sustaining, underneath, above,
The mighty wings, the song-filled heart of Love ;
And know all other songs, all other wings,
Are but dropped feathers and dim echoings.
     I dream — I dream of wings.

I HAD A FRIEND

I had a friend ; — in happy hour
We vowed beneath the almond flower
To tread one path, — there came a day
(Was the fault mine ?) — he missed the way.
     Ah, well-a-day !

I had a friend; — 'neath cloudy skies
I saw the sunshine in his eyes
And deemed it constant; — came a night
(Was the fault his?) — the dark was light
  To the eyes' night.

I had a friend; — his heart was pure,
Strong was his arm, his spirit sure;
We loved as friends do; — well-a-day!
I only know — we missed the way.
  Whose fault, I pray?

AMORICIDE

Was need of so much cruelty
 Even if he must be slain?
Could'st thou not murder decently:
Let him with arrows piercèd be;
 Or stabbed with swords amain?

Could'st thou not his young lips well slake
 With the bitter hemlock lees;
Could'st thou not burn him at the stake;
Or smother when he should awake; —
 Any or all of these?

But bitterer than poisoned cup;
 More cruel than the sword;

Thou bad'st him at thy board to sup,
Then snatched the ignoblest weapon up,
And slew Love with a word.

NOCTURNE

Night is the death of the day,
  Death is the night of life:
E'en as the cloud-wreaths may,
  (Leaving the still stars rife,)
  The clouds of passion and strife
Fade at sun-setting away:
Night is the death of the Day,
  Death is the night of Life.

The moon is the soul of the Night,
  But the soul of Day is the sun:
Darkness is undone light,
  And light is the dark undone:
  Sun- and moon-light are one
To the eye of unsealèd sight:
The moon is the soul of the Night,
  The soul of Day is the sun.

Love is the moon of Death,
  The sun of Life is Love:
Borne on its silver breath

The soul to the Soul above
Hath sped like a homeward dove
When the gold west darkeneth:
Love is the moon of Death,
The sun of Life is Love!

BE SATISFIED

Be satisfied! Love is not given in vain.
The poor parched earth is greener for the rain
The unasked heavens lavish; though earth tried
Long time and strove against it and denied
Her freshened flowers, her ransomed fields of
    grain;
The rain hath saved. And so, for all its pride,
Perchance unloved of thee a heart had died.
               Be satisfied!

Love on; until for Love's sake thou disdain
All things less lovely; so to love is gain,
Yea, is great gain. Though all the world de-
    ride
And hope grow weary, still, whate'er betide,
Love on, high heart! for thou shalt yet attain
Thy heaven, and denials put aside.
               Be satisfied!

CONSECRATION

Though Fame my own name had decreed
Imperishable, high-enrolled,
The human heart is one indeed,
My own heart's throbbing life hath told;
And while that heart beats high and bold,
To thee, O sorrowing World, I'll live,
Leaving the laurel leaf and gold,
All — all is thine I have to give!

Though Love, with measureless rich meed
Of warmth and light my life enfold,
Could I forget thy bitter need,
Sad World, whose unkissed lips are cold?
Poor World, like unkinged Lear of old,
Can love thy suffering state retrieve?
Thy daughter's heart shall naught withhold,
All — all is thine I have to give!

A QUEST OF THE GRAIL

Three knights, from distant lands afar,
Through frost and fire and gale,
From Southern Cross to Northern Star
They journey fast, they journey far,
They seek the Holy Grail.

They wander 'neath an alien sky,
    They may not pause nor rest;
Long, weary leagues they've journeyed by,
Long, weary leagues before them lie
    Who go upon this Quest.

And as beneath the palms they came
    Beside a tropic sea,
Each named his best-belovèd's name,
Each praised his best-belovèd's fame,
    Her pride and chastity.

The first knight said : " Earth hath not seen
    Another half so bright
As she, my Lady and my Queen,
Whose lightest smile I'd die to win,
    Whose frown doth make my night.

" The proudest and the purest thing
    In all Earth's broad domain,
Men's eyes behold her, marvelling,
Virtue so wraps her, as a king,
    His ermine free from stain.

" She stands as high and white apart
    As the snow mountains be,
And Love grows faint to try his art,
He hath no power to touch her heart,
    So proudly pure is she.

" And when I kneel to touch her hand,
    So slender, chill, and fair,
I seem the lowliest in the land,
And all my heart within to stand
    Death-smitten with despair.

" So forth I wander far and wide,
    Long lands I cross, strange seas I sail,
For haply he might mate her pride,
And haply he might call her bride,
Who hath no peer on earth beside, —
    The finder of the Grail."

The second spake: " Until the sun
    Shall fail and stars grow faint,
My steadfast faith is pledged to One,
No queen, more like a holy nun,
    My Lady and my Saint.

" No queen, in very sooth, is she
    To whom my vows are given ;
Not earthly proud like thy ladye,
Enwrapped in sweet humility,
    Pure as the souls in Heaven.

" Her mild blue meditative eyes
    Look strangely on our Earth ;

They long to seek communing skies ;
And so she liveth, angel-wise,
  Not as of common birth.

" And when I humbly kneeling touch
    Her robe with lips of love,
My heart grows still and faint o'ermuch,
My earthly passion shows as smutch
    To this white, heavenly Dove.

" Therefore I wander restlessly,
    I search the world, — I may not fail ;
For he alone her purity
Shall deem a worthy knight to be,
    Who finds the Blessèd Grail."

The third : " I have a Love," he said,
  " Her chosen knight am I ;
Her knight, yea, were I live or dead,"
(He took the helmet from his head.)
  " Since hers I live or die.

" Her heart encloseth all my heaven,
    Her honour is my own,
Her love unto my love is given,
Her life from my life shall be riven
    By cruel Death alone.

" No queen nor nun, she takes no thought
    For pride or chastity ;
She loveth, — more she hath forgot ;
She loveth, — more she knoweth not ;
    Yea, Christ, she loveth me !

" Her thoughts are all nobility,
    Her ways are ways of truth,
She walketh high, and fearlessly
She fronteth life, and tearlessly
    Her large eyes fill with ruth.

" She holdeth out warm hands to all,
    Her great heart overflows,
Her feet stay not lest they should fall,
No stains on her white robe appall,
    She hears a voice — and goes.

" She is not proud, — as queens are proud ;
    Not pure, — as nuns are pure ;
Her heart to Heaven she hath not vowed,
No human claim hath disallowed
    That Heaven doth endure.

" But when her eyes in my eyes shine,"
    (His own grew sweet and clear.)
" And when her arms about me twine
I know myself a Knight divine
    Above reproach or fear.

" And when her lips to my lips cling,"
    (He knelt upon the ground.)
" And when I clasp her, worshipping,
Oh, then I know myself a King
    Anointed, yea, and crowned!

" Her knight, — her favour in my crest,
    My heart beats strong and high,
Tireless, I neither stay nor rest,
I go upon my holy Quest,
    I follow till I die.

" I follow to Earth's farthest shore,
    The stars above me rise and pale ;
She will not love me less nor more,
Her love was freely given before, —
    I seek the Holy Grail."

" Now shame on thee, Sir Knight ! " cried one,
    " And shame on thy ladye !
Never beneath the blazing sun
Was lady-love so lightly won
    Since days of chivalry."

And " Shame on thee ! " the second knight,
    " And thy light love lightly given ;
Who for his lady need not fight
The shame is on them both aright,
    No Champion, thou, of Heaven."

Full fast they ride in scornful wise,
    In plumes and glittering mail;
The third, — he lifted up his eyes;
Lo, deep within the dying skies,
Where gold on gold the sunset dies,
Glow within glow, he saw arise
    The Rose of Heaven, — the Grail!

II

ITALY

A multitudinous stir and melody
  Of whispering leaves ;
Of olive boughs the subdued silver revelry
Held in the blue, and outside, fretting audibly,
  A wind that grieves ;
A perfume of warm violets in the air,
  Beneath and everywhere ;
A glimmer of dim marbles, rich and rare
  And marble-cold ;
The scent of Tuscan mould
Upbreathing where the crowding violets be
    Remindingly ;
A subtle, troubling something, faint and fair,
  Delight, — despair ;
A bird-song ; a far bell ; a drowsing bee ;
A murmur and a motion ; a caress
Of sun and air ; a touch, a tenderness ;
A smile that runs from Heaven down to me ;
A music and a silence —
    Italy !

SONGS OF ARNO

I

TWILIGHT

It is the hour when Arno turns
　Her gold to chrysoprase;
When each low-hanging star outburns
　Its faint, mysterious rays,
As from the prison of faery urns
　Which faery hands upraise.

It is the hour when life's constraint
　A moment's ease is given;
When Earth is like a holy saint,
　Stilled, sanctified, and shriven,
And the deep-breathing heart grows faint
　To be so near to Heaven.

II

MOONLIGHT

Oh, Arno lies in light afloat,
　The light moon floats a-near;
Her silver sheen, where close I lean,
　O'er Arno's breast streams clear;
Soft breathes a violin's low note, —
　I bend my soul to hear.

Oh, Arno shines, and sets within
   Her ripples all atune!   .
Hushed Earth and Heaven, as lovers even,
   Commingle in a swoon;
The light streams from the violin, —
   The music from the moon.

IN A MEDICEAN GARDEN

I know not why, but when the night is still
And nightingales are pouring out their heart
From the ilex-shadowed thicket 'neath the hill, —
When the soft fingers of the moonbeams part
Light   leaves,   whence   streams   the   hidden
   melody, —
My listening heart grows faint, my dim eyes fill,
Slow tears from under heavy eyelids start,
As drops fall from drenched flowers, resistlessly.

Garden and grove grow dim; they change and
   fade
Like their pale lords, the vanished Medici;
They are the phantomed shadows of a shade,
It is not night, nor earth, nor Italy;
And that which sings within the silences, —
I know him well, — no singer of the dark,
No alien bird, no foreign minstrel he,

But mine own unsung western-carolling lark,
Triumphant.singer of the farthest day,
Carolling earth, heaven, and Italy away.

I've heard him in the New World wilderness
Singing, sad nightingale, not notes like thine,
But plenteously poured forth like joyous wine
From an overflowing chalice. Loneliness
And sorrow were not then; the sunny plain
Filled and ran o'er with the melodious rain
Of music, and the golden-spacèd air
Trembled with happiness fine-felt and rare ;
While over, over, over, high above
Went lilting still the med-lark, love and love,
And joy and passionate joy and ecstasy.
O singer and O song, return to me !

I've known him fling such strains to so far height
Purple Sierras shook beneath their veil,
And golden poppies drank the liquid light
As down the molten music dropped and fell
Quivering, in notes of fire. O nightingale !
Thou art a silver singer, canst delight
Sad-hearted dwellers in the sad Old World,
With pallid chaplets of sweet song impearled
Upon a string of silence ; but too pale,
Too wan for me thy passion ; far too faint

The thrilling of thy melancholy plaint;
Thou art but love in sorrow, — I have heard
Love's self sing westward from a golden-throated
  bird!

WALT WHITMAN

O'er Tuscan hills I heard it breathed,
  And up the olive slopes it ran,
  And then the laurel all began
Singing of brows once laurel-wreathed;

Of bards whose vanished voices fill
  The resonant, deep valleys yet;
  The laurel never can forget,
Such echoes tremble through it still.

But I, — I let the laurel pass,
  And pass, the dim Etrurian land;
  Far louder sing within my hand
The voiceless syllables of grass.

Your music keeps its mighty ring,
  O ancient groves of Tuscany!
  But tenfold eloquent to me
The common herb One taught to sing.

Green art thou, laurel overhead,
  Yet sombre to this tiny blade,
  And some one says that he who made
The grass and me to live, is dead.

It may be true, — for Italy
  Hath seen the night of many a sun;
  Thou, O my Country, hadst but one,
If set, how dim thy light must be!

It may be false, — the sky's as blue,
  The ilex hath not dropped a leaf
  Nor Earth put off a rose for grief,
And yet, for all, — it may be true.

Unruffled, silver olives wave,
  Loud sings the laurel where I pass,
  But louder still I hear the grass, —
The grass, new-growing on a grave.

MEMORY

I watched the almond blossoms blow
And whiten the warm earth below;
  "Even so," I said, "they used to fall —
The still, white blossoms of the snow —
  In my first, earliest home of all;
  And I, a child, would watch them fall
In my New England, long ago."

I watched the petals of the snow
Whiten New England's breast; " And so,"
  I said, " I've seen my almond trees
  Snow down their blossoms when the breeze
Blew soft, as breezes used to blow
In that sweet season long ago
  In the dear Land of Sundown Seas."

A dweller in a distant star,
  Watching new worlds fade and arise
  Down the long vistas of the skies,
Shall I still yearn, with eyes afar
  And mists of memories in those eyes,
  " In my old earthly paradise,
Where all my lost belovèds are,
  Even so I watched earth's fireflies."

NEAR THE CARRARAS

The violets of mountains ! — such they seem;
Pale purple visions in a purple dream;
Faint, fading noonday violets, or again
Wet violets, after rain.
Blooming above the stone-pine's crooked stem,
Whose forest is but greensward unto them,
While the Ligurian sea breaks here alone
To feed the roots of the eternal stone.

A few years past, I thought our Earth had not
On her broad breast (that breast so thickly
strewn
With graves of hearts) a more memorial spot;
Remembering how the purple waters bore
The Prince of Song and laid him on the shore
With sob of wave and the slow breakers' moan.
I deemed these marbles' white when Angelo
came.
Seeking his prisoned Titans, caught the flame
Out of that Heart of hearts laid at their feet,
And blossomed into all these violets sweet
To be his deathless chaplet evermore.

God is our witness, if a God there be,
How He hath fashioned us all mystery.
Not less to-day is Shelley's song to me,
But Life, the Poem, is more than poesy.
Far have I fared, much seen with these eyes'
sight:
The white Alps flashing back their awful light,
Soft shadow of the Apennine's piny height,
And skiey needle of the Dolomite,
Only to learn how little these can be;
How little of itself the eye can see!
Have I not learned, — who look with longing
eyes

Across two worlds to where their shadows rise—
The Mother Mountains of the golden West;
Earth's highest heights for me, loftiest and love-
    liest,
The Mother Mountains ! — in whose shadow
    deep
No poet, but a mother, fell asleep.

ON THE SHORE

Grey skies bend down the narrow strand
    From the dim horizon's marge ;
Grey waters break on the greyer land
    Carrara holds in charge.

And " Lo," I said, "there doth as wide
    And salt a misery
My soul from other souls divide
    As these bitter waters be.

" And lo," I said, " there are heaped as high
    The mountains of my woe,
Till their tops, like these, pierce in the sky
    And my life lies crushed below."

Then, purple over the purple sea,
    Sails rode into my sight,

With wings set free where the port should be
　As birds to their nest at night:

Then purple clouds came folding them down
　Like birds at night to their nest,
And over Carrara's brow afrown
　A star stood still to rest.

And " How," I said, " if as ships set sail,
　Thou too on thy misery
Rode forth and gave to the driving gale
　Thy ships of sympathy?

" And how," I said, " if as clouds that rise
　Thou too on thy heaped-up woe
Set the mountains under thy feet — thine eyes
　In the skies beyond the snow ? "

Then silver waves 'neath a silver moon
　Crept, kissing the silver sand ;
And Carrara changed to a phantom soon,
　Guarding a gossamer land.

And " Now," I said, " I am glad for the sake
　Of the bitter seas that roll ;
For sailing their waters I will make
　My port in every soul ;

" And now," I said, " I am glad of the height
Of the mountains reared so far
That from their pinnacles this night
My soul hath touched a star! "

IN SANTA CROCE

They have lived and died : souls unto which my
own
Must show as a taper would when matched
with stars ;
They have left their impress upon every stone
That Florence wears ; and Florence not alone,
They shook the cage of the world and rent its
bars.

And after theirs my little life is set,
My feeble days and unfulfilling years :
Strange that the Earth should patiently forget
Suns whose last beams make bright her fore-
head yet
And suffer such as I to fill their spheres !

But since I am : accepted of the Earth
And heir of Titans, — dare I doubt it true
Me too the Universe has given birth ;
My soul, as theirs, has meaning, purpose, worth,
And its own work which Dante could not do ?

IN ROME

Thou standest in white robes, apart and high,
  And soldierly, a young priest militant,
  With flame-lit brow of the hierophant
And apostolic fire in thy dark eye ;
Proud, calm, and far removed from earth thou
    art,
  Pure priest of God, pure minister to man,
  Who, by the virtue laid upon thee, can
Atone the sins of which thou hast no part, —
Guiltless thyself, absolve the guilty heart.

No fault is in thee ; all attracts, all charms ;
  And yet before I trust my soul to thine,
  Stand there and answer this, thou priest
    divine :
Where are the children should be in those arms ?
O man of woman born, made Man alone,
  Where is the Woman on thy heart should
    rest,
  The head that should be pillowed on thy
    breast,
The equal soul that should complete thine own ?
O priest of Heaven ! — what heaven hast thou
    known ?

IN A ROMAN GRAVEYARD

I

AT SHELLEY'S GRAVE

O singing star! O voice of song! O soul
Which had the high, harmonious heaven for
    goal!
Lark which outsang the nightingale and past
As love outwearieth sorrow at the last,
And music, discord; ever-gentle spirit,
Which this here-lying dust did once inherit
And with a plenitude of life inform;
That life, that light went out in wreck and storm,
To rise again in an eternal sky
Of love and fame. The clouds are gathered by
Which, living, did o'erhang thee dark and thick,
Making breath, sorrow. The heart so over-
    quick
Lies cold beneath this stone; from age to age
Shall colder hearts make here their pilgrimage,
Kindling, as at the embers of a shrine,
Fire from the inextinguishable fire of thine,
Still warmer, cold, than any living is:
They shall make pilgrimage to thee for this
And for thanksgiving, for when men have
    blessed,

Praised, thanked, and loved all poets, then, thou
    best
And best-beloved of poets and of men,
They shall kneel here and love and bless again,
Paying with tears of love the debt they owe
For gift of all of heaven earth can know.
The highest gods own lowliest offerings,
So even I hither a gift may bring ; —
O Heart of hearts ! disdain not thou mine own
Laid with a violet upon the stone.

II

AT THE GRAVE OF KEATS

Child of all sorrow, and the younger brother
Of all the children of the divine Mother,
Take pansies for remembrance, — these and tears
In which thy name hath been writ through the
    years
Thou hast lain here in daisies ; — oh, not thou,
But all that earth could coffin ! Didst thou
    know —
Who felt the daisies grow above thee dead,
Thyself among the living, it is said, —
Didst thou know, dead, how many and how
    white
The snow bloomed daisies o'er thee yesternight

And flung them free o'er Rome? Strange daisies
    these
To grow in Roman grass, 'neath Roman trees.
Memorial flowers, — such I think they were ;
Pale, daisied ghosts felt long ago astir.
What brought them back I guess not ; — might
    it be
The selfsame mystery would bring back thee
One single hour to take the late remorse,
The love and pride sprung from the very source
Of the old hatred's bitter jealousy, —
An hour to take back these, — oh, might it be !
An hour, Adonaïs, from thy star,
Then back where all thy brother poets are.
We would not keep thee from them, — youngest
    Light
Of all the host wherewith dull earth is bright ;
Earth loves thee now, and Heaven must love, —
    else why
Snow daisies on thee from the very sky ?

III

BYRON

Thou dost not lie at Rome, my Byron, where
Thy brothers keep a tryst with sun and air
Of the eternal summer ; yet think not

Because of absence thou art there forgot
By those who lay the flowers dewy-wet
With tributary tears — sweet violet
And pansy — on two graves where should be
    three.
Who lays a pansy lays a thought for thee,
Beloved for all thou suffered first, then sung.
From out thy quivering heart-strings, overstrung,
Were swept the passionate great strophes first;
For anti-strophe, splendid tears outburst
Like torrents from a storm-cloud thunderous.
O Stormy-Cloud of poets ! so it was
Thy heart thou mad'st thy harp, thy woes the
    wind,
Thy music was the music of mankind.
For this, — for all thy greatness and thy wrong
And for thy sorrows baptised o'er in song,
Take all men's reverence, homage take, and
    praise,
For thou didst ever crave laurel and bays ;
But for thy human need,— poor heart !— take too
Sweet human pity — rosemary and rue.

SOUTHERN CALIFORNIA

Virgin of lands; the youngest one,
Whom last of all the dying Sun
      Delays his death to bless,
Daily bequeathing thee a dower
Of golden fruit and golden flower, —
      Crown for thy golden tress;

O sweet and dear, and ever-near,
Whose voice is always at my ear,
      Whose vision in my sight;
The youngest Mother's youngest born! —
In dreams my tired feet and worn
      Have trod again thy height;

Where mocking-birds sing all night long
And cañons lift and lift the song
      And strike the echoes up
To where the vestal yucca stands,
Swinging aloft in slender hands
      Her snowy incense-cup.

Or where the morning hath unfurled
A million poppy-petals, curled
      Beneath the shadowing dark,
And laughs to see to the morning skies
From every golden heart uprise
      A liberated lark.

Then shyer singers hold their breath
And listen, as one listeneth
    To a sudden Angel's voice,
The while the rosy valley flushes
And grove and garden blossoming blushes
    As each were the singer's choice.

And in the empire of the Rose
A splendid royal mandate goes,
    To put the purple on!
Who hath not seen that court-attire,
That cream and gold, that snow and fire,
    The Rose he hath not known.

Still-stepping Noon hath touched her eyes
And Earth, a sleeping beauty, lies
    With just-stirred, fragrant breath;
So drowsy hours she lieth dreaming
Till Dusk, his starry eyes a-gleaming,
    All eager hasteneth.

His first light kiss hath thrilled her heart
And like a bride's her sweet lips part
    To plight a willing troth;
So fair! — Day lingers to behold
The happy Dusk her form enfold,
    And Night surprises both.

Night; — O my Western Night! — what word,
What fancy suits thine undisturbed
    Serenest majesty!
Only the mute pen laid aside,
Only dumb lips, eyes wet and wide,
    Deep Night, can witness thee!

Whether in darkness, softer far
Than dusk; or lit with every star,
    Low-dropping lamps of light;
Or flooding into silver noon
Mid-dark, with thy intense white moon,
    None mates thee, perfect Night.

So, land beloved, all day, and then
All dreaming night and day again
    My heart wins back to thee;
Fashions some shape of thee forgot,
Some sweetest place, where I am not
    And where I fain would be!

CALIFORNIA OF THE SOUTH

The land is a garden of glamour, where passes
Each breeze on its wandering way to the sea,
And, prodigal, scatters the sweets it amasses
From orange groves, yielding their stores tenderly,

To be breathed back again to the tremulous
  grasses
Through which Zephyr ranges; — a light lover,
  he !

'Tis the garden of Eden; high hedges enclose it
Of lime and of cypress; a still Spirit rests
'Neath the veil of the mountain, (the hushed
  silence shows it)
And he broods the sweet valley to sleep on his
  breast.
This is a sanctuary; — every bird knows it,
And knows the broad landscape was made for
  his nest.

For hark how the hedges and bushes are ringing
With madrigals !   Mark how the jubilant trees
Are budding with birds and a-blossom with sing-
  ing ;
And look ! from each spray a small singer of
  glees
Is trilling and thrilling, his skyward song fling-
  ing ; —
Sure, Italy's skies are not bluer than these !

Here rain in swift showers soft tropical flowers
Sweet somnolent scents on the tropical air ;
Lavish roses have reared them a riotous bower,

Flaunting crimson and gold their gay gonfalons
  flare,
And the heart of each rose and the heart of each
  hour
Shows the last-bloomed the rarest, where each
  still was rare.

This is the land of the poet's desire;
This is the Beautiful's indwelling place;
Land of the new dawn and late sunset's fire,
Lo, she laughs like a child in the grim East's face!
And a thousand years shall be born and expire
Ere her youth shall have dimmed its immortal
  grace.

THE ROSE GARDEN

I stroll my garden through, where blaze
  Rose myriads such as Persia knows;
Lingering I pause and dream and gaze; —
In this rose world by rosy ways
  My life first blossomed to its rose.

And amorous of this great glow
  And perfume of the rose-filled space,
I loiter, linger, come and go,
And lean and breathe and bend me low
  Above each tropical flushed face.

These austral skies, these austral airs
  Have taught the Rose and me to bloom;
And who for any other cares
When once the flower of life he wears
  And breathes the flower of life's perfume?

Yet, grateful lover, while I bless
  The land wherein such flower grows,
Dear Land! I love thee not the less
That where thy rose ranks wave and press,
Amid a million, I caress
  This lowly, white, old-fashioned rose.

Such, rooted in New England's rock,
  Her humble dooryards used to frame;
And I am of New England stock:
Out of her sturdy granite block
  Sinew and blood and brain I came.

Though austral suns more richly wake
  Mine and the Rose's blood to start,
Yet where these throbbing millions take
The eye with splendour, here I break
This white rose for New England's sake
  And give it room upon my heart.

THE POPPY FIELDS

I know how just this morning light will trace
    Each golden face;
And how this selfsame beam strike boldly up
    Each glittering cup;
And how this breeze lift the wide, shining sea
    Up bodily,
And then in golden waves on the broad plain
    Let fall again.
The mountains will be palest amethyst
    Through a purple mist;
The valley will be blossoming white and pink,
    More than I think;
Almonds and peaches will have decked their hair
    With garlands rare;
And birds will be on every blossomed bough
    Carolling now.
Now will the lark his dropping music fling,
    (I'm listening!)
Heaven will stretch down two tender arms, and
    Earth
    Laugh low for mirth,
And where there was desire will be peace,
    And then increase
The summer long of Heaven upon Earth,
    And new heavens' birth,

And songful silences and silent song,
        The summer long.
But just to-day all that joy will be holden
        In poppies golden ;
It will be brimming o'er their cups aglow
        In a way I know,
And shining up the hillsides glimmeringly,
        In mists ; — ah me !
I've seen it, and I shall not see for years.
        These are the mists — not tears.

THE YUCCA

O mystic flower ! O white and glorious one !
Clad splendidly in raiment snowy fair,
Swinging thy censered bells in perfumed air,
Thine upraised head held statelily ; — alone
On heights so stern the very deer would shun
Such perilous solitudes ; no foot may dare,
Only uplifted eyes — to track thee there,
White dweller in the regions of the sun.
O great, sweet flower ! a flower-like soul I know,
Whose heights are loftier, lonelier still than thine ;
Whose spotlessness outsuns the spotless snow ;
Whose radiance through the infinite space doth
        shine,
Till lesser souls held fast to earth below
Raise love-lit eyes unto the Flower divine.

III

Unto my Love ! — these songs of love and sing-
    ing ;
To my Love's heart, — where my heart's love
    goes winging,
These songs of wings ; if folded there to rest,
I seek no other heaven ; — these, no nest.

THE LARK

You heard the lark: O love, what late lark sings
    In faded fields and meadows flowerless?
    They are all gone; the year was powerless
To hold them; Spring has flown and they were
    Spring's.

Was the note sweet? — dropped like a falling star
    Into the silence trembling to receive
    The molten passion: burden did it leave
Of sorrow, or dead joys that heavier are?

Love, it was last year's lark and last year's song
    (O faithful!) — echoing still in lonely heart:
    Memory that note a thousand times shall
       start, —
'Twas Love's, and both to the lost year belong.

Go east or west, sail far, it matters not:
    Still sings within the dim, sweet chorister
    Of half-remembered hours: the messenger
From dear, dead days that will not be forgot.

How will it sound, that haunting voice we know,
    Through the long years? — a requiem for
       hopes dead;
    A dirge for lonely hearts uncomforted;
For uncrowned lives, low monotone of woe?

Soul of my soul! — mayhap 'twill bend its wing
And thrill its jubilant song o'er lips that kiss,
O'er hearts that break with unimagined bliss,—
O love, O love, — God grant it so may sing,
The blessèd lark!

ONCE IN A WAY

Once in a way if Love mistake
And wing a bitter dart,
Shall I for that fond Love forsake
And for each errant arrow make
A quiver of my heart?

Ah, no! the sun shines through the murk,
Love bursts the bonds of pain;
No evil in Love's eyes can lurk,
Love slept, — another did the work;
Hail, Love, awake again!

LIFE, LIFT UP THY CURTAINS

Life, lift up thy curtains;
Love has entered in;
How he came I know not;
If with martial din, —
If with glittering pageant,
Or golden trumpet's blare, —
I saw not, or I heard not,
I only know, — he's there!

IF HE SHOULD COME

If he should come, who is most dear,
My heart on his would throb to lie ;
If he should speak, my heart, to hear,
Would cease its throbbing straight, — so die ;

Then should he sorrowing kiss my eyes,
Being dead, I'd enter Paradise ;
But should he kiss my lips, I'd spurn
Paradise all and swift return.

AFTERTHOUGHT

I gave the jewel, but withheld
    The casket from his hand :
And yet the casket was excelled
    By thousands in the land.

The jewel I so light resigned,
    So lightly bade him wear, —
Go search the world, and never find
    A second like it there.

Strange niggard I, so to mistake
    False values for the true :
Bring back my jewel, love, or take
    The worthless casket too.

VAINLY I WOULD DENY

Vainly I would deny thee,
  So dear, so dear thou art grown:
    How should my heart refuse thee?
    'Tis losing all, to lose thee,
And anguish to deny thee.
Then let all else go by me,
  Love, I will be thine own.

Ah, didst thou ever doubt me,
  This moment shall atone!
    Ask what thou wilt, Love, — prove me;
    What's life — death, when I love thee,
Fold thy dear arms about me,
(Oh, foolish heart to doubt me!)
  Love, take me for thine own.

CONFESSION

Thine, oh, most wholly thine! — I would not
    say it
  An hour since when thy pleading lips were
    near;
That kiss of thine — I would not then repay it,
  Lest all my soul should tremble through it,
    Dear.

Thine and forever thine ; — I would not show it,
  Raising such telltale eyes to thine ;
Not for the world, — ah! should'st thou know it,
  How could I rule this heart of mine ?

Thine ; — and I would not for the world undo
    it ;
  Though Heaven itself stood open at my
    prayer,
Not for one single blessing would I sue it,
  — Forsaking Heaven for thee, — lo, Heaven
    is there !

THE WOMAN

I

AMBITION

To have enriched his life by one sweet hour ;
By one glad hope to have o'ergilt his grey ;
Chased but one darkening shadow from his day ;
To his long winter given one single flower ;
And bride-like to have brought him but the
    dower
Of one brief moment's bliss, which would not
    stay
But even as he clasped it fled away
And left behind not e'en a memory's power ;

To know that once, through me, he drained de-
    light;   ·
That once, because of me, his earth was heaven ;
And in the compass of one day or night
By gift of mine was infinite rapture given ; —
O crowned reward !   O rich indemnity !
Paying life, death, and all eternity.

II

THE QUESTION

Could I forget if I had given
    So greatly and so tenderly ;
    If I had been the world to thee ;
With thee had entered Love's high heaven ;
    In perfect glad surrender free
    Had given thy lips their will of me,
    In thine arms touched Love's mystery, —
Oh ! if life's self had thus been riven,
        Could I forget ?
Forget ! — when lips with lips had striven
    For passionate supremacy ;
    When souls had mingled bodily ; —
Oh, not till bitterest death had driven
    Love, life itself from memory,
        Could I forget !

III

PREVISION

Some night, — God knows when we its grace
    shall see ! —
I shall lie long awake while thine eyes sleep,
And from my own the happy tears will creep
Softly to hide them where the kisses be
Among the curls my lips touch tenderly ;
I shall feel them stir with each deep-throbbing
    leap
My heart gives feeling them, and I shall weep
And tremble tenfold more for ecstasy.
Because that after bitter years apart
And desolating doubt, this end should be, —
Thy kisses on my lips, — (how the tears start !)
Thou wearied out with joy upon my heart,
And I too weak and faint with bliss to move,
An hour since made a wife, — thy wife, O love !

IV

CONSUMMATION

Now let earth fade, — it is but earth ;
    Let Heaven prove a lie, —
' Tis only Heaven ; let life, let birth
    Be dead ; — let death too die !

For I have outlived earth and heaven,
　Outvanquished death and life,
Whose lips the immortal kiss have given
　That seals the woman — wife.

Love made me mistress, bride, and wife
　To his divinity ;
Mother I shall be, (Love gives life,)
　To Immortality.

FANCIES

A thousand sunbeams dancing and a thousand
　roses glancing,
And a thousand bird-songs thrilling, trilling,
　gladsome o'er the lawn,
Revelry in place of quiet ; all a mad midsummer
　riot ; —
　　O Sun, — if thou wert gone !

A thousand hopes soft-singing and a thousand
　joys upspringing,
And a thousand thousand happy dreams, like
　blushing roses red ;
Throbbing heart aglow with gladness ; life but
　the divinest madness ; —
　　O Love, — if thou wert dead !

WITH ORANGE BLOSSOMS

Thou'lt never know! I sent thee blossoms white
And perfect as an earthly tree may bear;
Wet with fresh dews, and odorous as fair;
So pure, so fair they need not dread the light
Of thine eyes on them. Happier than I,
I sent my flowers where I might not go,
And close beneath the petals' perfumed snow
And sheltering leaves, safe-hid my heart doth
    lie; —
       Thou'lt never know!
Poor heart! I placed it there, wet through with
    tears,
Trampled and torn and stained, unfit for thee,
Unfit; and yet — poor heart! — so filled with
    prayers
For pardon, passionate grief, and purer love,
I dared to send; wilt thou receive? Ah, me!
I heaped the heavy flowers so close above
       Thou'lt never know.

THE WISH

I'd be a temple for my love
    Fitly to worship in;
An altar with a shrine above,
    His reverence to win;

A lamp undimmed, to draw his eyes
    Upward forever;
A saint, that he might idolize
    Less purely never.

Alas! no saint am I; my light
    Is all untrimmed;
My altars ravished, and by profane rite
    The fair shrines dimmed.
A temple this? — nay, he will scorn and go;
    Meet so it is!
And yet, — I'll bring fresh flowers still to show
    It still is his.

THE STARS OUT OF THE SKY

The stars out of the sky, O God!
    The moonlight off the sea;
The light out of the dawn; the dawn
Out of the world; all suns withdrawn;
    Blithe still the world should be.
But, pitying God! — that night of day
    When sun and moon and stars shall shine
    In vain for any eyes of mine,
With all things else, — and Love away.

THE HOME-HELD TO THE WANDERER

Farewell! — the outward blowing breeze,
O traveller, is thine; new seas,
New continents that border these
   Be thine!
Farewell! — and yet the truth might prove
'Tis you who stay, 'tis I who rove,
Even I, the home-held thrall of love,
   The rooted vine.

To me the little miles of men
Your feet shall press and press again
   Would scarce a journey be;
The suns and moons your eyes shall bless
In cities old and wilderness
Wax pallid to the measureless
   Vast orbs that burn for me.

Full gloriously, full gloriously
   My great sun goeth down;
Full solemnly, full solemnly
   Upriseth my calm moon;
And be the night or dark or bright
My heart it knows what constant light
   Of stars shall shine on me.

SEA DRIFT

How little, ah, how little seem
The shallow voyages men dream,
     Unto my mighty sea;
The heights they climb, how low, how dim,
To those I hourly climb with him; —
     My Alps, my Italy!

The secrets of all Europe's skies
Lie hidden in a pair of eyes,
     Where daily I explore;
I need but lift and turn my own,
    But lift and turn my own to see
    More than the Orient's mystery,
Age-old, new-born, waked from the stone:
     The Sphinx and something more.

On wilder wastes, in every mood,
My frail barque gives her to the flood,
     Unmeasured as it rolls
Down to the seas more dark, more deep,
Where the uncharted currents sweep
     To the unventured poles.

And when upon a purple shore,
With uplooped sail my barque I moor,
     And night o'ertaketh me,

Not strange to my adventured keel
The sands of any land shall feel,
Nor reck I though its heights reveal
  At dawn — the shoreless Sea.

SEPARATION

The world is full of farewells! Is it so?
 Not to the dying alone, but to all
Who feel the throbbing of this pulse of life
 Must these sad farewells fall?

I hold thy hand; thine earnest eyes, O friend,
 Look full assurance from thy soul to mine,
Nor can they shine nor darken forth one thought
 But my heart shall divine.

Dear dreaming lips, thy varying mould betrays
 The changing mood, as words were faint to do,
Yet is there not an echo of thy voice
 But shakes my pulses too.

How am I grown so wise that lips and eyes,
 Down-dropping lids, the colour in thy cheek,
Hold each a language more familiar, dear,
 Than tongues of others speak?

I'll tell thee : there are threads so subtly spun
  Eye cannot seize them nor the touch divine,
Yet strength is naught beside them, and they run
  From thy soul unto mine.

Strong as the stars and flower-tremulous,
  Of various span, attuned in perfect way,
An infinite harp, whose thrilling strings life-
    swept
  Supernal music play.

And thoughts and feelings, ne'er so dimly stirred,
  Flash their swift messengers these paths along,
And smite the slumbering harp-strings till they
    wake
  Into majestic song.

Each faintest throbbing of thy spirit's life,
  Transmitted, breaks in music into mine ;
And mine can breathe no feeblest note but stirs
  The answering chord in thine.

Death cannot rend these beating strings, nor
    Time,
  The Universe itself not give them pause,
Only a spirit disobedient
  To its own spirit laws ;

Only a soul disloyal to itself,
　Leaving the highest harmony it knew,
Breaking its music for discordant ends,
　Shatters its harp-strings too.

And this is separation, — this alone ;
　There is no other ; farewells have no force
For those who keep unchanged through chang-
　　ing lives
　This voiceless intercourse.

What though to-morrow tossing waves and
　　leagues
Of alien land shall hide thy face from me,
And hands can feel each other's clasp no more
　Though stretched imploringly ; —

Shall we therefore be parted ?   Is there power
　To bind the spirit willing to be free ?
Say no, a thousand times ! — nor Time, nor Space,
Earth's darkest gloom, nor Heaven's divinest
　　grace,
Life's sombrest shadow, nor Death's awful face,
Hell, — nay, not God Himself in highest place
　Can stay my soul, — my loving soul from
　　thee.

SEA THOUGHTS

By night, by day,
Fast on its way,
Sails steadfastly the noble ship:
High foam the waves its prow about,
And in and out
And round about
The grey gulls wheel and curve and dip.
League upon league their unwearied wings
Beat the wide air, the waters call;
And on they speed, strange eager things,
Winged expectations,
Starved aspirations,
Fed on the crumbs the ship lets fall.
If in some frozen gale those wings should tire
Till bird by bird went down in storm and death,
Lived but in one the last, faint lingering fire,
Methinks that one, still deathless in desire,
Would lay its throbbing life down on the deck.

Strong soul and great!
Ship bearing freight
For all mankind, speed on thy starward way!
Fast in thy wake my hopes and longings,
Winged dreams and fancies thronging,
Follow and live upon thy life each day.

Though far the course and bold the track thou
  steerest,
Too far, too bold, for untried wings like mine,
And one by one each thought that tracked the
  nearest,
Each hope the dearest,
Fade, fall, and sink beneath the trackless seas,
I'll save me still: — folding its pinions whitely,
The wingèd wisdom, — Love, which long upbore,
Shall droop him to thy heart ; lying there lightly
As the dusk lies upon the daylight nightly,
Flight of thy flight, I'll reach the farther shore !

TO A TWILIGHT BREEZE

Sweet wandering breath, how knewest thou to
  find
    My Florentine far nest ?
How many twilights, days, and dawns combined
    Fulfilled thy quest ?

What wide, fresh prairies of unbeaten air
    Hast thou o'er-run
To end thy course upon my cheek ? — sweet,
  where
    Was it begun ?

What miles and miles of perfumed, shadowy
    places
    Saw thee depart,
Stooping how oft to steal with soft embraces
    Some shy flower's heart?

Cool uplands, meadows, fragrant orchard-closes,
    Still darting over;
Scorning the lofty trees to kiss — here roses,
    And there a clover.

Then speeding o'er how many wayward seas
    The happy ships,
Art come from mine own land? — whisper, dear
    breeze, —
    When didst thou leave *his* lips?

O HAPPY FIELDS

O happy fields!   O fields with light o'er-run
Where golden poppies catch the glowing sun;
Fields by a thousand perfumed breezes swept
Which late sweet company of orange blossoms
    kept;
A million tiny lives swarm safe among you;
The joyous lark long, long hath oversung you,
Wooing his love ; each creature hath a mate
In your glad range, — not one is desolate,
    O happy fields!

None desolate, ye fields; not I! not I!
Not though a thousand envious spaces part
My love and me; on thoughts more swift to fly
Than wingèd lark, I hover close about him;
I love him so that I can live without him,
Brooding him ever closer in my heart,
Ye happy fields!

THE MESSAGE

From gardens green I send, most Dear,
  Twin messengers to thee;
This leaf of olives centuries sere,
New grass, new grown with the springing year;
  I bind them, send them over sea
  From gardens of dead Medici.

Bidding them say: — " When Life was fleet
  And Time was young — (that time is fled.)
Such grass grew under courtly feet,
Such olives caught the murmurs sweet
  Of lovers' lips long dead;
  The leaves know what they said.

" For Love is younger than the grass
  And than the olives older;
Before the olives were, Love was;

Love will be, when the olives pass ;
  And when the living grass shall moulder
Love will but only spring up bolder."

LIFE COMES, LIFE GOES

Life comes, Life goes, brief hours and days
  Consume its scanty breath ;
Love comes but once and henceforth stays,
  He knows nor Life, nor Death ;

Who deem they once have known Love's shape
  And seen the phantom go,
Have seen a mime Love's aspect ape,
  They never saw Love, — no !

WITH FOLDED HANDS

Is there no more ?   Is there no more ?
When love has spent its utmost store
Of all to do, to give, to say, —
Has love no way ?   Has love no way ?
Love has a way, — with folded hands
Across the sea, across the lands,
All done, all said, all spent, all given,
Still to convert its hell to heaven.

Though nothing it can bate or save
Of suffering, anguish, or the grave ;
Though helpless, motionless, must see
The far belovèd's agony ;
Then gives Love most, then spends most, where
He sits denying to the air
And sun and stars his own despair ;
Not in his closet's secret space
With fast-locked door looks in its face ;
For well Love knows, with traitor eyes
Did he the coward recognise
Winged through locked doors the knowledge
flies,
And seas, skies, continents apart,
Shall find out the belovèd's heart.
An inner light within the light
Smite the belovèd's day to night ;
Sound waves beyond the mortal ear
Be messengers of mortal fear ;
The palpitating ether be
A porter of his treachery.
All this Love knows, and knows as well
Brave word or deed will not befit
Without the brave heart back of it
With courage at its inmost cell ;
That earth hath not a solitude
Sufficing for a fainting mood ;

And whoso deems himself alone, —
Allows his heart one secret moan,
Betrays his own! — betrays his own!
Or lets his soul to be afraid,
He is betrayed! — he is betrayed!
Love knows Love never is alone.
O loving heart, remember this!
These need; — thy hands are emptiness.
These suffer with no power to bless:
Shalt thou curse, then, and die?   Poor heart!
Rise now, play thy heroic part;
Nor play it merely, — thou must be
In that heart's core the deity.
Fold thy wrung hands, mute lips and pale;
Sit still and love; all else may fail,
This shall avail!   This shall avail!

MARCH

O dearest month, — most dear of all
    The treasure of the year!
Grey are thy skies, thy robe a pall,
Few flowers thine, and yet I call
    Thee dear, March, and most dear.

A poor pale month they name thee oft,
    And harsh and ill of face;

But I will praise thee till I die,
I will proclaim from earth to sky
 Thou art the month of grace.

What need hast thou of violets,
 Spring's bird, or Summer's flower?
The fairest things the sun begets,
Sun-golden dawns, golden sunsets,
 Are poor beside thy dower.

For when thy dooryards made faint mirth
 With snowdrops pale and few,
A soul, — O say a star ! — had birth
In heaven, forth it sped to earth
 Through illimitable blue.

It bore Spring's resurrection flower,
 A lily flecked with gold ;
Summer's delight, sweetness, and power ;
The glory of the October hour,
 To kindle March's cold.

It came ; and all things sensitive
 Foreknew it for divine ;
It came, a human life to live ;
It made itself a gift to give,
 A light set for a sign.

March! when they call thee bleak and poor,
  A barren month and wild,
And when they count May's jewels o'er,
June's wealth, each jealous sister's store,
  Point only to thy Child.

The blossoms of a thousand springs
  Make sweet his summer eyes;
Above his heart, with folded wings,
A nightingale forever sings,
  Forever a lark replies.

Shall bloom when all earth's flowers are dead
  The flower of his fame;
When all Earth's birds are dumb and fled,
A nightingale shall sing, and shed
  Fresh music with his name.

Earth hath a million flowers that swell
  The pageant of the year;
Amid thy snows one rare seed fell,
Bloomed one white, perfect Immortelle, —
  Should I not call thee dear?

TEACH ME THY WAY

Teach me thy way, — thy better way, Love,
　Lest I fall utterly from thee;
I cannot tell how dark and far I stray, Love,
　Bend down the light of thy dear eyes on me.

Stretch out thy hand, — thy saving hand, I
　　pray, Love,
　That I may clasp and cling and climb thereby;
Healing is in thy touch, my own hand may, Love,
　Grow pure and white if close in thine it lie.

Let not thy heart, — thy pardoning heart forget,
　　Love,
　How weak am I, how strong all else beside;
Keep but my name on thy dear lips and yet,
　　Love,
　Shielded and safe am I, whate'er betide.

Thou art my star, — the star my dim eyes see,
　　Love,
　Where like a tired child I roam apart;
My only light! — draw me, I pray, to thee,
　　Love;
　Oh, fold me safe at last within thy heart!

www.ingramcontent.com/pod-product-compliance
Lightning Source LLC
Chambersburg PA
CBHW022149020726
47496CB00008B/2627